TRUMPET

Cameron Mackintosh Presents
Boublil and Schönberg's

Selections From
Les Misérables

A Musical by
Alain Boublil & Claude-Michel Schönberg

Lyrics by Herbert Kretzmer

based on the novel by VICTOR HUGO

Music by CLAUDE-MICHEL SCHÖNBERG
Lyrics by HERBERT KRETZMER
Original French text by ALAIN BOUBLIL
and JEAN-MARC NATEL
Additional material by JAMES FENTON

Orchestral score by JOHN CAMERON
Production Musical Supervisor ROBERT BILLIG
Musical Director JAMES MAY
Sound by ANDREW BRUCE/AUTOGRAPH

Associate Director and Executive Producer
RICHARD JAY-ALEXANDER
Executive Producer MARTIN McCALLUM
Casting by JOHNSON-LIFF & ZERMAN
General Management ALAN WASSER

Designed by JOHN NAPIER
Lighting by DAVID HERSEY
Costumes by ANDREANE NEOFITOU

Directed and Adapted by
TREVOR NUNN & JOHN CAIRD

THE MUSICAL SENSATION
1987 TONY® AWARD BEST MUSICAL

CONTENTS

ISBN 978-0-7935-4899-6

ALAIN BOUBLIL MUSIC LTD.

EXCLUSIVELY DISTRIBUTED BY
HAL•LEONARD®
CORPORATION
7777 W. BLUEMOUND RD. P.O. BOX 13819 MILWAUKEE, WI 53213

T0050944

Visit Hal Leonard Online at
www.halleonard.com

AT THE END OF THE DAY

Trumpet

Music by CLAUDE-MICHEL SCHÖNBERG
Lyrics by HERBERT KRETZMER
Original Text by ALAIN BOUBLIL and JEAN-MARC NATEL

BRING HIM HOME

Trumpet

Music by CLAUDE-MICHEL SCHÖNBERG
Lyrics by HERBERT KRETZMER and ALAIN BOUBLIL

CASTLE ON A CLOUD

Trumpet

Music by CLAUDE-MICHEL SCHÖNBERG
Lyrics by HERBERT KRETZMER
Original Text by ALAIN BOUBLIL and JEAN-MARC NATEL

DO YOU HEAR THE PEOPLE SING?

Trumpet

Music by CLAUDE-MICHEL SCHÖNBERG
Lyrics by HERBERT KRETZMER
Original Text by ALAIN BOUBLIL and JEAN-MARC NATEL

DRINK WITH ME
(To Days Gone By)

Trumpet

Music by CLAUDE-MICHEL SCHÖNBERG
Lyrics by HERBERT KRETZMER and ALAIN BOUBLIL

EMPTY CHAIRS AT EMPTY TABLES

Trumpet

Music by CLAUDE-MICHEL SCHÖNBERG
Lyrics by HERBERT KRETZMER and ALAIN BOUBLIL

A HEART FULL OF LOVE

Trumpet

Music by CLAUDE-MICHEL SCHÖNBERG
Lyrics by HERBERT KRETZMER
Original Text by ALAIN BOUBLIL and JEAN-MARC NATEL

I DREAMED A DREAM

Trumpet

Music by CLAUDE-MICHEL SCHÖNBERG
Lyrics by HERBERT KRETZMER
Original Text by ALAIN BOUBLIL and JEAN-MARC NATEL

IN MY LIFE

Trumpet

Music by CLAUDE-MICHEL SCHÖNBERG
Lyrics by HERBERT KRETZMER
Original Text by ALAIN BOUBLIL and JEAN-MARC NATEL

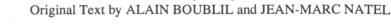

rall.   a tempo

2

f *piu mosso*

mf

rall.

A LITTLE FALL OF RAIN

Trumpet

Music by CLAUDE-MICHEL SCHÖNBERG
Lyrics by HERBERT KRETZMER
Original Text by ALAIN BOUBLIL and JEAN-MARC NATEL

ON MY OWN

Trumpet

Music by CLAUDE-MICHEL SCHÖNBERG
Lyrics by ALAIN BOUBLIL, HERBERT KRETZMER, JOHN CAIRD,
TREVOR NUNN and JEAN-MARC NATEL

STARS

Trumpet

Music by CLAUDE-MICHEL SCHÖNBERG
Lyrics by HERBERT KRETZMER and ALAIN BOUBLIL

WHO AM I?

Trumpet

Music by CLAUDE-MICHEL SCHÖNBERG
Lyrics by HERBERT KRETZMER
Original Text by ALAIN BOUBLIL and JEAN-MARC NATEL

PLAY MORE OF YOUR FAVORITE SONGS

WITH GREAT INSTRUMENTAL PLAY ALONG PACKS FROM HAL LEONARD

Ballads
Solo arrangements of 12 songs: Bridge Over Troubled Water • Bring Him Home • Candle in the Wind • Don't Cry for Me Argentina • I Don't Know How to Love Him • Imagine • Killing Me Softly with His Song • Nights in White Satin • Wonderful Tonight • more.

00841445	Flute	$10.95
00841446	Clarinet	$10.95
00841447	Alto Sax	$10.95
00841448	Tenor Sax	$10.95
00841449	Trumpet	$10.95
00841450	Trombone	$10.95
00841451	Violin	$10.95

Band Jam
12 band favorites complete with accompaniment CD, including: Born to Be Wild • Get Ready for This • I Got You (I Feel Good) • Rock & Roll – Part II (The Hey Song) • Twist and Shout • We Will Rock You • Wild Thing • Y.M.C.A • and more.

00841232	Flute	$10.95
00841233	Clarinet	$10.95
00841234	Alto Sax	$10.95
00841235	Trumpet	$10.95
00841236	Horn	$10.95
00841237	Trombone	$10.95
00841238	Violin	$10.95

Disney Movie Hits
Now solo instrumentalists can play along with a dozen favorite songs from Disney blockbusters, including: Beauty and the Beast • Circle of Life • Cruella De Vil • Go the Distance • God Help the Outcasts • Kiss the Girl • When She Loved Me • A Whole New World • and more.

00841420	Flute	$12.95
00841421	Clarinet	$12.95
00841422	Alto Sax	$12.95
00841423	Trumpet	$12.95
00841424	French Horn	$12.95
00841425	Trombone/Baritone	$12.95
00841686	Tenor Sax	$12.95
00841687	Oboe	$12.95
00841426	Violin	$12.95
00841427	Viola	$12.95
00841428	Cello	$12.95

FOR MORE INFORMATION, SEE YOUR LOCAL MUSIC DEALER,
OR WRITE TO:

HAL•LEONARD CORPORATION
7777 W. BLUEMOUND RD. P.O. BOX 13819 MILWAUKEE, WI 53213

Visit Hal Leonard online at **www.halleonard.com**

Disney Solos
An exciting collection of 12 solos with full-band accompaniment on CD. Songs include: Be Our Guest • Can You Feel the Love Tonight • Colors of the Wind • Reflection • Under the Sea • You've Got a Friend in Me • Zero to Hero • and more.

00841404	Flute	$12.95
00841405	Clarinet/Tenor Sax	$12.95
00841406	Alto Sax	$12.95
00841407	Horn	$12.95
00841408	Trombone	$12.95
00841409	Trumpet	$12.99
00841410	Violin	$12.95
00841411	Viola	$12.95
00841412	Cello	$12.95
00841506	Oboe	$12.95
00841553	Mallet Percussion	$12.95

Easy Disney Favorites
13 Disney favorites for solo instruments: Bibbidi-Bobbidi-Boo • It's a Small World • Let's Go Fly a Kite • Mickey Mouse March • A Spoonful of Sugar • Toyland March • Winnie the Pooh • The Work Song • Zip-A-Dee-Doo-Dah • and many more.

00841371	Flute	$12.95
00841477	Clarinet	$12.95
00841478	Alto Sax	$12.95
00841479	Trumpet	$12.95
00841480	Trombone	$12.95
00841372	Violin	$12.95
00841481	Viola	$12.95
00841482	Cello/Bass	$12.95

Favorite Movie Themes
13 themes, including: *An American Symphony* from Mr. Holland's Opus • Braveheart • Chariots of Fire • Forrest Gump – Main Title • Theme from *Jurassic Park* • Mission: Impossible Theme • and more.

00841166	Flute	$10.95
00841167	Clarinet	$10.95
00841168	Trumpet/Tenor Sax	$10.95
00841169	Alto Sax	$10.95
00841170	Trombone	$10.95
00841171	F Horn	$10.95
00841296	Violin	$10.95

Jazz & Blues
14 songs: Cry Me a River • Fever • Fly Me to the Moon • God Bless' the Child • Harlem Nocturne • Moonglow • A Night in Tunisia • One Note Samba • Satin Doll • Take the "A" Train • Yardbird Suite • and more.

00841438	Flute	$12.95
00841439	Clarinet	$12.95
00841440	Alto Sax	$12.95
00841441	Trumpet	$12.95
00841442	Tenor Sax	$12.95
00841443	Trombone	$12.95
00841444	Violin	$12.95

Lennon and McCartney Solos
11 favorites: All My Loving • Can't Buy Me Love • Eleanor Rigby • The Long and Winding Road • Ticket to Ride • Yesterday • and more.

00841542	Flute	$12.99
00841543	Clarinet	$12.99
00841544	Alto Sax	$12.99
00841545	Tenor Sax	$12.99
00841546	Trumpet	$12.99
00841547	Horn	$12.99
00841548	Trombone	$12.99
00841549	Violin	$12.99
00841625	Viola	$12.99
00841626	Cello	$12.99

Movie & TV Themes
12 favorite themes: A Whole New World • Where Everybody Knows Your Name • Moon River • Theme from Schindler's List • Theme from Star Trek® • You Must Love Me • and more.

00841452	Flute	$10.95
00841454	Alto Sax	$10.95
00841455	Tenor Sax	$10.95
00841456	Trumpet	$10.95
00841458	Violin	$10.95

Sound of Music
9 songs: Climb Ev'ry Mountain • Do-Re-Mi • Edelweiss • The Lonely Goatherd • Maria • My Favorite Things • Sixteen Going on Seventeen • So Long, Farewell • The Sound of Music.

00841582	Flute	$11.95
00841583	Clarinet	$11.95
00841584	Alto Sax	$11.95
00841585	Tenor Sax	$11.95
00841586	Trumpet	$11.95
00841587	Horn	$11.95
00841588	Trombone	$11.95
00841589	Violin	$11.95
00841590	Viola	$11.95
00841591	Cello	$11.95

Worship Solos
11 top worship songs: Come, Now Is the Time to Worship • Draw Me Close • Firm Foundation • I Could Sing of Your Love Forever • Open the Eyes of My Heart • Shout to the North • and more.

00841836	Flute	$12.95
00841838	Clarinet	$12.95
00841839	Alto Sax	$12.95
00841840	Tenor Sax	$12.95
00841841	Trumpet	$12.95
00841843	Trombone	$12.95
00841845	Violin	$12.95
00841845	Viola	$12.95
00841846	Cello	$12.95